To Donna
in love & grace
for your friendship!

The
Jewels
Of
Here
And
Now

Ragini

Additional Books
by Ragini Elizabeth Michaels

Unflappable – 6 Steps To Staying Happy, Centered, & Peaceful
No Matter What (2012)
Conari Press, San Francisco, CA

"WOW! What a work of wisdom Unflappable *is! It weaves wisdom from many traditions for those who aspire to live a mystical and meaningful life while staying centered and grounded. It is a profoundly practical guide for anyone dancing with the tides of change, complexity, immensity, and the uncertainty of these times."*

—**Joel Levey, Ph.D.,** author of *Luminous Mind* and *The Fine Arts of Relaxation, Concentration, Meditation*

The Wildly Quiet Presence of God: Musings of A Modern
Marketplace Mystic (2007-2015)
Create Space Independent Publishing

"Whispers from the Divine heart to yours . . . The musings of this modern day mystic open the part of you that is beauty, love, and being . . . Each poem and image is unique but wonderfully complementary. The Wildly Quiet Presence of God *is visually exquisite. What a rare treat!"*

—**Jay Schlechter, Ph.D.,** author of *Reminders of Love,* and *Chasing Bliss.*

<u>Lions In Wait – a road to personal courage</u> (1993)
Facticity Trainings, Inc. Seattle, WA

—**Anglo-American Book Co., England,** *The book is genius; and very beautifully written."*

<u>Facticity – a door to mental health & beyond</u> (1991)
Facticity Trainings, Inc., Seattle, WA

"Facticity is beautifully done and filled with meditations and suggestions I'm sure will be helpful to practitioners and counselors and general readers. After reading your book, I am left with great respect for your work and its deep and spiritual integration."

— **Jack Kornfield, Ph.D.,** Psychologist & Author of *Seeking the Heart of Wisdom* and *No Time Like The Present*

Contributing Author

<u>Coaching For Female Entrepreneurs – How Life Coaching Can Improve Your Bottom Line</u> (2017)
Global Management Inc.

The Jewels

Of

Here

And

Now

Awe, Reverence, And
Ever Deepening Gratitude

Ragini Elizabeth Michaels

ISBN-13: 978-1986414821
ISBN-10: 1986414825

Library of Congress Control Number: 2018903241

Printed by CreateSpace, an Amazon.com Company
CreateSpace, Charleston, SC

Dedication

To my Outer and Inner Master—
with awe, reverence, and ever deepening gratitude

"You must live in the present,
Launch yourself on every wave,
Find eternity in each moment...."

Henry David Thoreau

Table of Contents

Forward

In the pages that follow, you will experience a human heart opening to the sweet inner beauty of life.

The owner of this particular heart is Ragini Elizabeth Michaels, a wise soul with a sharp mind, as if uncannily tuned to seeing through the contradictory paradox in everyday life. I mention this only because Ragini's work is almost always sprinkled with mystical insights – and this book is no exception.

But that is not what you will enjoy most about this compilation of poems. No, if you are like me, what will move you most about this work is the plain talking, fun and vulnerable tone. And the way Ragini conveys her deep reflections so effortlessly and unselfconsciously. Tucked charmingly into this poetry are the many faces of Earthly paradox, whispered to us from the deep chambers of the human heart.

In *Every Day at Least Once or Twice,* one of the 48 poems shared in this volume, Ragini writes "I never would have thought / taking time / to just *be* could be / a part of my / cosmic job / description." This compilation of poetry is testament to the beauty we unleash when we learn to open ourselves to the full and cosmic meaning of our work here on Earth. To witness the unfolding of a human soul is rare privilege. And with this sweet and poignant collection, you hold just that: an intimate window into a wise and lovely heart, opening to the timeless beauty in which it beats.

I hope you enjoy these poems even half as much as I have.

Gideon Rosenblatt, Writer, The Vital Edge
Seattle, Washington, March 2018

Acknowledgements

I give my heartfelt thanks to my family and friends who encourage me to share these musings that somehow arise amidst the gifts and challenges of my journey.

A special thanks to Suzie and Steve Dardas for their role in making this second book possible. Also, gratitude to my wonderful Sufi friend, Basira K. Johnson, whose publishing and editing knowledge was invaluable, and to Nadine Shanti for her patience and kindness in proofing a book of poetry that is free to break all the rules of good grammar. And a special thanks to Gideon Rosenblatt for his kind words and his commitment to creating a better world with AI that is infused with love and consciousness.

Although I took a few of these photographs, the majority of images are from Pixabay.com and MorgueFile.com. This book would not be as lovely without the beautiful and often stunning contributions of the photographers who offer their work, free of attribution and cost. These artists do not ask for acknowledgment. But I would like to honor their creativity and unselfish sharing of their work. To that end, I have listed Photo Credits at the back of the book. If you find an artist you'd like to follow, I've included a link to their work on Pixabay.com. or MorgueFile.com. I offer my apologies to the cover artist as I was unable to re-locate your work on Pixabay.com.

Last, I want to acknowledge the guidance that pours forth from my still haphazard visits to the Here and Now—and from my Inner Master who obviously loves me more than I can begin to comprehend.

April 2018

Dear Fellow Traveler,
As promised, *The Jewels Of Here And Now* is the first companion
volume to *The Wildly Quiet Presence of God* (2015).

I hope you enjoy these 48 offerings chosen from what is now 144
musings written over the course of 12 years. Each musing is again
paired with a beautiful image that often inspired the contemplative
inquiry.

When honesty reigns supreme, I know I haven't a clue what terms
like 'soul', 'consciousness', and 'illusion' refer to. In fact, my traveling
companions are often hopelessness and helplessness, and I feel
unable to grasp any clarity at all. Unfortunately, I often interpret this
as my personal failing.

But it's only then another dimension of this amazing and mysterious
life enters the playing field, making it clear my beautiful mind is *not*
going to be privy to the clarity it desires. This realization opens the
door to something resting deep within my interior. And the notions
of awe, reverence, and ever deepening gratitude leap from concept
into real life experience – of course, changing everything.

If you believe you're not savvy enough to catch a glimpse of Truth,
Love, and Freedom, you're probably right. But there is *something*
within us that can. May that 'something' help you, as it is helping me,
through the challenges of each day with a laugh, a tear, or perhaps
just a goofy little smile.

Much love, Ragini

Whispers Of Joy

Delicate Flower

Delicate flower—
Did you know your presence is enough
to lift my heart to the heavens—

And curve my body into an
astonishingly
prayerful
bow?

When A Flower's Beauty

When a flower's beauty
Is a real show stopper—
It is obvious—
Even to the uninitiated eye.

I wish I believed *my* beauty could stop the show—

But all I usually see are flaws.

I feel better when I forget about
Performing and instead, dive into my heart.

That's when my unquestionable beauty
Becomes free to just run hog wild!

Too Many Insights

Too many insights and
Understandings at one time
Can overwhelm me.

Although I adore these showers of clarity,
They can disrupt my balance.

That's when I want to lean
Against a beautiful tree—

And take refuge
In the power of its
Whispered silence.

When The Sun Shines So Brightly

When the sun shines so brightly,
I feel a bit shy.

Not sure why, really.

But I honor
The pull to hide out a bit—
Not be quite so brazen in
Revealing

My
Beauty.

Maybe it's because
It took me
So long
To
Find
It.

Maybe I just want to
Keep it close for a while—

And
Enjoy
Its
Wonder
All
By
Myself.

When My Eye Catches A Bird

When my eye catches a bird
Resting its entire body on the
Highest and skinniest limb of a tree,

I am struck with awe—
And an odd shiver of joy.

The next time I'm out on a limb,
I'm going to remember that bird—

And trust my capacity for equanimity
Will leap forth
And keep me balanced too.

I Used To Have A Bad Attitude

I used to have a bad attitude toward winter—

Until I realized it always played host
To the annual summit of birth and death.

Winter gives birth and death room
To run in wild abandon
Through the cold and dark—

Spreading their hues of reddish wine
And green beginnings of luscious futures
Yet to come.

I imagine them huddling together—
Lost in their mutually thrilling

Vortex of creativity.

It must be a pretty joyous collaboration.

It certainly results in
The bountiful and
Enticing
Sophistications of design
We call spring.

Every Once In A While

Every once in a while,
I hear a symphony playing.

It can be some pretty stunning stuff.

But there are never any musicians around!

And no one else
Seems to take notice.

Perhaps it's the
Flowers singing – or the
Ocean harmonizing with the tides.

I think everything in life
Has a voice.

Even me.

Maybe it's my own
Divine melody playing
just
for
my
ears
to
hear!

Wouldn't that
be
ever
so
sweet?

Once I Learned To Not Be So Afraid

Once I learned
To not be so afraid of the dark,
Things changed.

Oh, I have respect for the darks' muscle and might.

But it seems that
Love For The Divine
Has even more.

Wish I'd known
It was
That simple
A long time ago.

I would have switched my
Allegiance earlier—
And
Gotten
Drunk on joy
A lot more often.

Winter Captures
A Shimmering Image

Winter captures
a shimmering
image
of her
private reflections
inside
the
frozen
landscape.

Quietly
she suspends
her eternal
dance
of
change.

This grants us
time
to
ruminate
on the grandeur
and finery
of
her
most
intimate
deliberations,
graciously
immobilized
in the
icy splendor of
exquisitely
simple
beauty.

There Is A Rightness
In This Design

There is a rightness
in this design—
Hiding in the delicious
juxtaposition of
perfect circle
and faulty square.

I suspect the stones
would reveal their secrets to me
if I could be quiet
for a while.

Then perhaps
I could learn

to create this
beautiful balance

Amidst
the
perfect
imperfections
of
my
own
life.

We Grumble At Transition's Annoying Presence

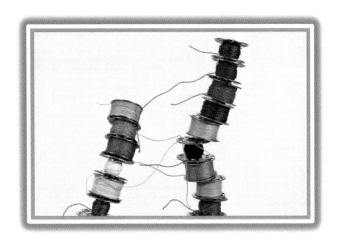

We grumble at Transition's
annoying presence—

Ignoring the
subtle beauty of Her handiwork.

She disentangles us from the
past while weaving translucent
threads of guidance to
a future not yet fully formed.

She might enjoy some thanks
for Her hard work—

instead of all our complaints
about the
inconvenience
and
disruption
She
so
lovingly
creates.

An Indiscriminate Eye Is Blind

An indiscriminate eye is blind
to the uniqueness of each flower
making up the bouquet.

Yet—isn't individuality the
intrinsic escort to all touting life?

I like to hold this notion as truth
and keep an eye out for my own
brand of specialness—

But I sure don't want to give up
my spot in the Whole
in order to find it.

In Plain Sight

The Heron's Magnificence

The heron's magnificence
hinders the eye from
noticing other things
also in plain view—

Like the ripples on the pond,
or the constantly changing compositions
of shadow and light.

Sometimes there is just
so much 'isness'
the eye can only
take it all in
by letting go of trying.

Sometimes
What's In Plain Sight

Sometimes what's in plain sight
is clearly calling for my attention—

But I'm hesitant.

I want to get closer and feel it up a bit—
get a sense of its texture—

Whether the surface is soft or hard—
whether my hand experiences its

weight as heavy or light—

Whether it's going to nourish, or is
something best to avoid.

My mind supports the notion that a
little exploration is prudent.

On the other hand,
my heart loves adventure—

It adores the surprise of
not actually knowing
what's coming next!

The little bugger usually wins out,
getting me into more trouble
than I care to admit.

But I must fess up—
I'm grateful
for its courage
and daring!

Following my heart means
I am rarely,
if ever,
bored!

Elegance

Elegance
Is hard to put into words.
But when it does appear—
Right before your eyes—
You immediately recognize
Its beauty and style.

I have the same experience
When I accidentally bump into the
Presence of what I'm told is the real me.

To my surprise, this 'me' is
Amazingly graceful—
And Incredibly Loving!

What Seems Messy At First Glance

What seems messy at first glance
can actually be
quite an array of order—

That is, if I take a step back
and embrace the notion of
a design hiding out in the chaos.

It's amazing what can be seen
by an astute eye
trained to flush out
disorder's hidden symmetry.

Every Day
At Least Once Or Twice

Every day, at least once or twice,
I get caught up in the idea that
I'm totally in charge
of my life!

A compulsion grips me
and I'm forced to try and
make something
happen—fast!

The idea I have this kind
of responsibility sort of
puts a damper on my
sense of freedom.

I'm so glad Wisdom
grabs my ear and
tells me to

Make my efforts, take action,
and then—

Relax and let things
be as they are.

It's kind of wonderful
when I remember I don't have
to constantly *do*.

I never would have thought
taking time
to just *be* could be
a part of my
cosmic job
description.

What a blessed relief
to know that my relaxing
isn't the same as
Atlas shrugging and
dropping the whole world
on its head.

My Longing To Be Still

My longing to be still
and just rest
calls to me more often these days.

The forest's silent aliveness
entices me
to simply sit down
and
do nothing for awhile.

I enjoy this activity of stillness
more than seems reasonably possible.

Perhaps nature is
instructing me once again

how to enjoy
the vastness
of
life's
small
moments.

When I Simply Refuse

When I simply refuse
to acknowledge
what is in plain sight—

Whether out of
stubbornness or ignorance—

Life can get a bit huffy.

That makes her boldly
place her offering
right at the tip of my nose.

In this case,
it seems best to wise up fast

And find the beauty
in her
presentation
right
then
and
there!

The Bud & Blossom

The bud and blossom
hang out
in perfect harmony—

Each waiting its turn to arise—and then disappear.

Wisdom likes to wrap itself
in the simple and easy—
Offering guidance and

direction in the most subtle
yet obvious way.

Isn't life a hoot?

What it wants to teach us
is always right there—
in plain sight.

.

We just have to
get brave enough
to reach out
and catch hold of what's there—

And
Then
Ferret
Out
The
Gems
Being
Offered.

It's Clear
No Two Yellow Peppers

It is clear no two yellow peppers
are the same.

Yet they are exactly the same
in all the important ways.

In fact, they're even the same as
red, green, and orange peppers—

Despite
their obvious differences.

If we could see people like peppers,

Don't you agree
the world
could be
an easier place
to
call
home?

Not Paying Attention

Not paying attention
To what's up
For my heart and soul
Usually turns into a big problem.

Being unwilling to take the next obvious step
On my journey
Just slows down my arrival
At the destination.

My heart and soul have little tolerance
For my rebellious shenanigans.

To speed things up, they often take my next
Learning and make it mushroom
Into a big drama—hoping I will then

Acquiesce to their desire.

Since my dislike of drama
Is quite intense these days,

It seems they've stumbled on
An excellent strategy.

Outer Reflections, Without Apology

Outer reflections, without apology,
Broadcast what is
Near and in plain sight.

Inner reflections, without regret,
Reveal how we make
Sense of things—

Good or bad—
Right or wrong—
Truth or lie.

It rocked my world
When I discovered

My reflections were not the final
Truth about reality.

I hadn't realized our perception of
The 'here and now' could be such
A personal creation.

Now that I know,

It's just a lot easier
To get along
With
Everyone.

My Eyes Love Anything

My eyes love anything
That will grab hold and magnetize their gaze.

But I'm a bit nosey.

What is this mysterious pull out to gain?

Perhaps Life just wants to
Capture our attention.

Apparently,

The 'why' of it
Is left for us

To
Cleverly
Surmise.

Glimpses

Of

Grandeur

How Does Nature Do It?

How does nature do it?

Such balance,
Such poise.

Such gracious
Demeanor.

I get a bit overwhelmed
Trying to
Take it all in.

Especially
When I
Open to the notion

I am
Also

A

Divine

Gesture

Gracefully

Unfolding.

When Life Creates Such Intricate Beauty

When life creates such intricate beauty—
So tiny and hidden deep inside
The heart of a flower—

Couldn't it also have created the
Same magnificence within me?

If you want to know if all this
Spiritual talk is just a lot of falderal—

It's a question worth
Contemplating quite seriously,
Don't you think?

The Waterfall Demands

The waterfall demands
To be heard.

It is so insistent,
Nothing else
Can garner my attention.

The same happens
When my soul
Parades its prowess
And drowns out all

Except its silent
Invitation to guidance.

I confess this is the most
Beautiful of sounds—
For once heard,
My heart
Can only bow
And say
'Yes".

When I Lose Sight Of Life's Magic

When I lose sight of Life's magic,
I deduce She's hiding out—

Like that aura of enchantingly soft
And captivating light embracing all
That dances to the
Tune of shape and form.

When She decides to peek out,
I leap up in delight—

And She graces my eyes
With the grand spectacle of Her presence

Touching everything
With Her wand
Of wonder
And
Marvelous
Design.

In The Outer World, Speed Is King

In the outer world, speed is king.
Everything needs to be done
Yesterday.

My inner world wants to
Make haste too—
But slowly, mindfully, wisely—
Everything free to unfold in its own time.

Gratifying both of these
Contradictory worlds is quite
The challenge.

But the more I reflect on this,
The more I glimpse the harmony
Hiding out between them.

I never considered that
Such an obvious
Impossibility
Could actually be
The real deal.

Earnestly

Contemplating A Rose

Earnestly contemplating a rose
Often evokes
A vast
Valley of silence.

What to say
When the efforts of
Exquisite design
And
Flawless fragrance

Fail to camouflage a beauty
And majesty

So grand
That it stills
Even
The most
Passionate
Heart?

Ever Notice How

Ever notice how
Each new season
Sends a scout
Ahead
Announcing
Its eminent
Arrival?

Amidst the
Opulence of fall's
Colorful vanity,

Winter's advent sneaks up—

And before you
Know it,
The trees
Begin to
Earnestly engage
In their yearly
Disrobing—

Somehow relishing
The revelation of
Their inimitable
Bare beauty,
Once again,
Before the sky's
Preordained admiration.

What Must It Be Like

What must it be like
To be so relaxed that you're willing to be
Vulnerable?

No thought for your
Surroundings or whether you'll
Achieve the desired
Approval of those
Around you?

It must be sweet and filled with
A delightful freedom.

That's where I'm headed—

Not sure when I'll set up

Housekeeping there—

But miraculously,
I somehow scored a daily
Visitor's pass.

Accident or kismet?

Think I'll go with good fortune
And just enjoy!

My Passion Doesn't Emerge Symmetrically

My passion doesn't emerge
Symmetrically—or organized
In any way.

It just splashes forth and
Rearranges itself according to
Where it lands.

This reflects the true heart
Of creativity—highlighting the
Angle that I'm just the
Instrument it so beautifully
Flows through.

I enjoy this enticing taste of
The Beyond—

Even though it's
Not a flavor my ego enjoys.

Ever Contemplated The Notion?

Ever contemplated the notion
That flowers & leaves
Are already perfectly formed
Before
They
Unfurl?

I have to trust
This is true
For any unfolding—
Including mine.

It helps me to relax.

Then I can savor the wonder
Of already being complete
While I
Keep working
To
Smooth
Out
Those pesky rough edges
Still
Hanging
Around.

Sometimes
When I Lose My Grounding

Sometimes
When I lose my grounding,
All I can do is wait
And be still—

But it's not a fallow time.
I encounter wonderful and
Engaging things—

Like the joy of rest—

The commanding call
Of silence as it summons sound—

The grandeur offered by what's in front of me
Instead of the ambitious
Possibilities
Yet to come.

Truth be told,
I'd rather spend my time
Seeing 'what is'—
Savoring those
Moments of freedom
From stress and striving.

But then again,
I still have to pay the rent.

So when the ground is once
Again beneath my feet,
Off I go—
Renewed and refreshed—
To gladly perform
The required dance of the day.

I Cried Loud & Long

I cried loud and long
When I discovered I was flying through
An empty sky.

I wept quietly
When I realized
My flight,
Each and every day,
Left no trace
Across the heavens.

Not a single
Motion of my journey
Disturbed the
Stillness
Of the blue.

But then,
I realized
How marvelous it was
That I was
Flying
At
All!

And oh—how I laughed
As I stumbled on
The impossible solidity of a
Groundless
Ground.

It was suddenly clear it had always been there,
Just beneath my feet,

Even though it was patently
Obvious to the naked eye
That
None
Was
There
At
All!

The Gifts Of

Letting

Go

I Was Taught Life Is A Very Serious Affair

I was taught life is a very serious affair.
There's a lot to do—and to become.

Fulfill your God given
Potential and then ... you'll be happy!

That made me a VERY serious person.

I tossed fun in the trash,

Declaring it an unworthy pursuit—

Despite not having a clue what fun was,
Or, how to find it.

Then one day, weary from the
Heaviness of it all, I decided to
Experiment—

To try letting go
Of being an egg head
And just laugh—

Really act silly and stupid for awhile.

And to tell the truth,
That was one of the
Most freeing and happy days
Of my life!

When I Let Go Of Fear

When I let go of fear,
My prowess and boldness
Naturally arise.

The past stretches out behind me,
Done
And now irrelevant—

With calm, I look the unknown
Future in the eye,

Confident I will
Master its challenges.

With the past and future

No longer
My captors,
I am free to simply
Rest, relax, reflect and respond.

And I have to tell you—

That
Is
The
Height
Of
Luxurious
Living.

Sometimes I Get Focused On Why

Sometimes I get focused on why—
Or who did the evil deed that
Messed
Up
My
World!

I can't let go until I've
Solved the mystery.

Like any amateur detective,
I often miss what's right in
Front of my face.

Curious how every single time
I forget to consider
My role
In fashioning the fiasco!

No Matter How Hard
I Hold On

No matter how hard I hold on—
Or how long—
Deep in my heart I know
All things eventually
Pass away.

I get it. Everything changes.

Time highlights

Life's insistence that
Nothing stay the same—

As well as my unwillingness to let go
And graciously welcome the new.

Obviously, I'm not wild
About life's agenda.

Everything races toward its next
Creative expression—
Leaving me in the dust
With arms foolishly wrapped around
What once was!

I suppose it's time to wise up
And look for security
Elsewhere.

If I honor my own ripening,
Perhaps contentment
Will come out of hiding
And grant me
A
Long
Desired
Audience.

Lust & Greed Have Always Been

Lust and Greed
Have always been my two favorite guests.

They adore pleasure
And taught me how to
Dance to the glorious rhythms
Of gluttony.

Lust luxuriates
In the sensual decadence of
Indulgence—and greed wants to make sure
There's always more to enjoy.

Sadly, I'm hooked on

The deliciousness of what these
Friends bring for dinner.

But here's the rub.
I also desire the taste of a higher love.

Lust and greed got a little anxious
When I stumbled on
The middle road
Of moderation.

I think
They know their time
As my favorite guests
Is almost up!

It's Hard To Embrace
The Idea

It's hard to embrace the idea that
Something is perfect
When it's obviously imperfect.

Yet, I've been told this
Conundrum is really quite
Simple to solve.

The wise ones say this:

"Let go of the notion of perfection."

When I do give it a try,
It's surprising how
Everything
Suddenly appears
Just as it is—

No comparisons,
No judgments,
No critiques.

But it's the funniest thing.

There's such a flawlessness
In that remedy that it will make you
Laugh out loud.

And I don't think you can get
Any more perfect than that!

I've Worked Hard

I've worked hard to be the
Most unique person possible—

Assembling myself to reflect
The amazing expanse of the
Peacock's tail—fanned out and
Flaunting its glory.

It was fun—although a lot of work
To assure everyone utter the
Ooh's and aah's I secretly
Wanted to believe I deserved.

But I'll share with you—
Privately of course—
Uniqueness is a totally bogus
Goal as it simply does not
Live up to its hype.

So I let it go and decided to
Invite humility out for dinner.

Don't know what humbleness
Really is—but it's got to be a
Lot less exhausting.

And I'm told,
It might free me
From the tiresome game
Of making life always about me!

I Don't Believe An Acorn

I don't believe an acorn
Has any concerns
About its future.

It's not planning, calculating, or
Assessing possibilities like I do.

I doubt it knows about the beautiful
Pre-designed oak tree sitting inside
Itself waiting to emerge.

No—the acorn is too wise for all that.
I bet it's just resting there—allowing
Things to unfold in their own time.

I'm going to follow the acorn's example

And let go of my worrying.

It's a big risk—but I'll just trust
Something equal to that mighty oak
Is also resting inside me.

When Pain Stabs At My Heart

When pain stabs at my heart,
Her staunch defenders—anger & hurt—
Rush forward
Forcing the heart to go cold.

As guardians of my tender emotions,
These warriors rally round me.

They grab my
Attention and wield powerful
Creative defenses that deflect
All ugliness and hate.

I appreciate their efforts—but, honestly?

I'd rather let my old school protectors
Go back to base camp for some R&R—

Then I'd place the reins of my attention
Back into the hands of my heart.

I much prefer the forgiving power of love.

It's warm and wonderfully cozy.

Plus, it's not nearly as demanding
As going to war.

I Enjoy A Little Adventure

I enjoy a little adventure
Now and then, don't you?

Still,
It does take
A bit of daring—

And stealth —
To pull it off.

I'm often too cautious and
Miss a lot of the fun.

I've found it's best
When I let go of

Any fear and trembling—

And just pretend I can
Embrace the escapade.

To be sure, it's a challenge.

But isn't that
Amazing taste of glory
What adventures are for?

Calendars Aside

Calendars aside,
Just when does fall end
And winter begin?

The leaves and raindrops know
When it's time to transition
Into a new adventure.

Their impeccable
Sense of timing
Frees them to unerringly
Engage in the
Daring act of ending the past,

And opening the door
To an unknown

New beginning.

I'm keeping my fingers crossed
I can find
That same
Flawless mastery
Inside of me.

This Life Is Definitely Juicy

This life is definitely juicy—
Always ready to bust wide open with wonder
And sweetness.

But to savor the delights of this
Liquid Joy of Being

I'm told
I have to drink up.

It's apparently mandatory to relinquish the safety of just
Contemplating the miracle.

Seems like a pretty high price to pay
For a sip of joy.

So just to be clear—

The taste of this incredible juice
Had better
Hit my taste buds
With such gusto,

They can't help but loudly sing

Blissful
Melodies
Of
Wildly
Passionate
Praise
All
Day
Long!

Photo Credits

Artists from Morguefile.com have MF behind their name. All others, excepting Ragini, are from Pixabay.com. To see more photos from any artist, write in their username after the last forward slash in the appropriate url: https://pixabay.com/en/users/
http://www.morguefile.com/creative/

Whispers of Joy...

1. Delicate Flowers – Did You Know? —Maialisa
2. When A Flower's Beauty—MichaelGaida
3. Too Many Insights—jplenio
4. When The Sun Shines So Brightly—Ragini
5. When My Eye Catches A Bird—Surku/MF
6. I Used To Have A Bad Attitude— Ragini
7. Every Once In A While—cocoparisienne
8. Once I Learned To Not Be So Afraid—xololounge/MF
9. Winter Captures A Shimmering Image—KarolynAnn/MF
10. There Is A Rightness In This Design—Ragini
11. We Grumble At Transition's—fotoblend
12. An Indiscriminate Eye Is Blind—Ragini

In Plain Sight..

1. The Heron's Magnificence—bones64
2. Sometimes What's In Plain Sight—HfHansen
3. Elegance Is Hard To Put Into Words—AngelaL_17
4. What Seems Messy At First Glance—vidiaviola
5. Every Day, At Least Once Or Twice—VICKYHEVIA
6. My Longing To Be Still—2690457
7. When I Simply Refuse—Ragini
8. The Bud And Blossom Hang Out—Ragini

About The Author

Ragini, most loved and appreciated for her work in Paradox Management, is also an internationally acclaimed trainer of Neuro-Linguistic Programming (NLP), Certified Life Coach and Personal Wellness Consultant, and accomplished Hypnotherapist with a background in Physiological Psychology.

 Her original work on Mystic Psychology and how it's relevant to our everyday lives, has received critical acclaim, taken her throughout America, Canada, Europe, and India presenting workshops and seminars, and evolved into her 8-week on-line training, *The Mystic's Wisdom: De-Coded.*

She is the creator of eight hypnosis/meditation Mp3's in two series—*Hypnosis To Heal The Heart & Soul* and *Hypnosis For Conscious Awakening*, author of four earlier books on paradox and mystic psychology, and founder of the Paradox Wisdom School, Seattle, Washington, 2000-2010, using the Enneagram to better surf our dual identity as both human and divine.

Her approach to spirituality stems from her diverse professional background, and over forty years personally exploring meditation and contemplation via Vipassana retreats, trips to India, years as a disciple of an eastern mystic, and more.

Upon finally owning her mystical bent, she began to share her experiences of exploring spirituality and the power of viewing mundane life problems with an eye for mystical guidance and insight.

You can visit her at **www.RaginiMichaels.com**. For more information and trainings, please email **rm@RaginiMichaels.com** or call **001 425 462 4369**.

Free Resources

Videos:

The Psychology of the Mystics (the foundation of Unflappable)
www.raginimichaels.com/unflappable/psychology-of-the-mystics/

Unflappable – 6 Steps To Staying Happy, Centered, & Peaceful No Matter What (Book Trailer)
www.Amazon.com/author/raginimichaels

The Wildly Quiet Presence Of God (Book Trailer)
www.Amazon.com/author/raginimichaels

The Beggar's Secret To Happiness (3 video series)
www.TheBeggarsSecret.com

Fun Videos: Issues People Bring To Personal Coaching
www.bottomlinecoaching.net/FreeFunVideos.en.html

Audio:

Moving From Fear To Love (audio series)
www.raginimichaels.com/move-from-fear-to-love/

E-book:

Two Liberating Points Of View That Dissolve The Desire To Argue
http://www.raginimichaels.com/opt-in-free-two-liberating-viewpoints/

Blogs:

Marketplace Mystic Blog
www.RaginiMichaels.com/blog

To Help You Help Others Blog
https://tohelpyouhelpothers.com/blog/

92854553R00073

Made in the USA
Columbia, SC
03 April 2018